Moses
Children's Leader Guide

Moses:
In the Footsteps of the Reluctant Prophet

Moses
978-1-5018-0788-6 *Hardcover with jacket*
978-1-5018-0789-3 *eBook*
978-1-5018-0790-9 *Large Print*

Moses: DVD
978-1-5018-0793-0

Moses: Leader Guide
978-1-5018-0791-6
978-1-5018-0792-3 *eBook*

Moses: Youth Study Book
978-1-5018-0800-5
978-1-5018-0801-2 *eBook*

Moses: Children's Leader Guide
978-1-5018-0802-9

Also by Adam Hamilton

24 Hours That Changed the World

Christianity and World Religions

Christianity's Family Tree

Confronting the Controversies

Creed

Enough

Final Words from the Cross

Forgiveness

Half Truths

John

Leading Beyond the Walls

Love to Stay

Making Sense of the Bible

Not a Silent Night

Revival

Seeing Gray in a World of Black and White

Selling Swimsuits in the Arctic

Speaking Well

The Call

The Journey

The Way

Unleashing the Word

When Christians Get It Wrong

Why?

For more information, visit www.AdamHamilton.org.

ADAM HAMILTON

MOSES

In the Footsteps of the
RELUCTANT PROPHET

CHILDREN'S LEADER GUIDE
BY SALLY HOELSCHER

Abingdon Press / Nashville

Moses:
In the Footsteps of the Reluctant Prophet
Children's Leader Guide

This book is printed on elemental chlorine-free paper.

978-1-5018-0802-9

17 18 19 20 21 22 23 24 25 26—10 9 8 7 6 5 4 3 2 1
MANUFACTURED IN THE UNITED STATES OF AMERICA

Contents

To the Leader

This children's leader guide is based on Adam Hamilton's book *Moses: In the Footsteps of the Reluctant Prophet*. This guide includes six lessons that take a look Moses' life and ministry. Children will hear about Moses' life and explore learnings from Moses' story that may be applied to their own lives.

The subjects for each of the six lessons parallel the subjects in the program's adult and youth studies. Because of this feature, families will be able to discuss, across age levels, what they have learned in each session.

The lessons in this guide, designed for children in kindergarten through sixth grade, are presented in a large group/small group format. Children begin with time spent at activity centers, followed by time together as a large group. Children end the lesson in small groups determined by grade level. Each lesson plan contains the following sections:

Focus for the Teacher

The information in this section will provide you with background information about the week's lesson. Use this section for your own study as you prepare.

Explore Interest Groups

In this section you'll find ideas for a variety of activity centers. The activities will prepare the children to hear the Bible story. Allow the children to choose one or more of the activities that interest them. Occasionally there will be an activity that is recommended for all children, usually because it relates directly to a later activity. When this is the case, it will be noted in the sidebar notes.

Large Group

The children will come together as a large group to hear the Scripture and story for the week. This section begins with a transition activity, followed by the story and a Bible verse activity. A worship time concludes the large-group time.

Small Groups

Children are divided into grade-level groups for small-group time. Depending on the size of your class, you may need to have more than one group for each grade level. It is recommended that each small group contain no more than ten children.

Younger Children

The activities in this section are designed for children in grades K-2.

Older Children

The activities in this section are designed for children in grades 3-6.

Reproducible Pages

At the end of each lesson are reproducible pages, to be photocopied and handed out for all the children to use during that lesson's activities.

Schedule

Many churches have weeknight programs that include an evening meal; an intergenerational gathering time; and classes for children, youth, and adults. The following schedule illustrates one way to organize a weeknight program.

5:30	Meal
6:00	Intergenerational gathering introducing weekly themes and places for the lesson. This time may include presentations, skits, music, and opening or closing prayers.
6:15–7:30	Classes for children, youth, and adults.

Churches may want to do this study as a Sunday school program. The following schedule takes into account a shorter class time which is the norm for Sunday morning programs.

10 minutes	Intergenerational gathering
45 minutes	Classes for children, youth, and adults

Choose a schedule that works best for your congregation and its Christian education programs.

Blessings to you and the children as you explore the life and teachings of Moses!

1. The Birth of Moses

Objectives

The children will:

• hear the story of Moses' birth.

• discover that God was at work in Moses' life through the actions of courageous women.

• explore ways to discover God at work in their lives.

Bible Story

The Birth of Moses
Exodus 1:8–2:10

Bible Verse

She named him Moses, "because," she said, "I pulled him out of the water."

Exodus 2:10b

Focus for the Teacher

Many years before Moses was born, an Israelite boy named Joseph was sold into slavery by his brothers. After many struggles, Joseph became second-in-command to Pharaoh in Egypt. Eventually Joseph was reunited with his family, and Joseph's entire family moved from Canaan to Egypt. Joseph's family, the Israelites, thrived in Egypt, and for a time they received special treatment because of Joseph's importance and standing. But times change—people die and new kings come to power.

At the beginning of the Book of Exodus we learn that after Joseph died, a king came to power who did not remember Joseph. Instead of granting special privileges to the Israelites, the king became afraid of them and made them slaves. Even after the Egyptians enslaved the Israelites, the number of Israelites continued to grow. The king decided population control of the Israelites, also known as the Hebrew people, was necessary. The king instructed the Hebrew midwives, Shiphrah and Puah, to kill any Hebrew baby boys who were born. Courageously, the midwives did not follow Pharaoh's orders. When Pharaoh asked the

> This story reminds us God is at work in the world.

midwives why they were letting the Hebrew baby boys live, they lied and told Pharaoh that the Hebrew women were giving birth without their help. Not to be deterred, Pharaoh decreed that all Hebrew baby boys must be thrown into the Nile River.

Into this hostile environment a Hebrew baby boy was born. His mother was understandably unwilling to follow the king's decree to drown her baby. Instead she hid him for three months. Presumably at this point the baby was too noisy or too mobile to continue to hide. So, the mother did end up putting her baby boy into the Nile River, but first she put him in a basket. Instead of drowning, the baby floated among the reeds in the river until another woman, who happened to be Pharaoh's daughter, discovered him. Pharaoh's daughter took pity on the child, whom she recognized as a Hebrew baby who was supposed to be drowned, and saved his life.

God was at work early in Moses' life through the actions of four courageous women. This story reminds us God is at work in the world. It also encourages us to consider how we are called to do God's work.

Explore Interest Groups

Be sure that adult leaders are waiting when the first child arrives. Greet and welcome each child. Get the children involved in an activity that interests them and introduces the theme for the day's activities.

Weave a Basket

- Give each child a bowl.
- Have each child make a series of cuts in the bowl from the rim to the bottom of the bowl, spacing the cuts evenly around the container. The exact number of cuts is unimportant, as long as there is an odd number of cuts.
- Invite each child to choose a color of yarn and cut a piece about three or four feet long.
- Have each child tie one end of the yarn tightly around one of the paper tabs of the bowl, near the bottom of the bowl, securing with a knot.
- Encourage each child to weave the loose end of the yarn through the slits in the bowl, alternating putting the yarn over and under the tabs.
- As the children weave, have them push the yarn toward the bottom of the container.
- If children reach the end of their yarn before finishing the basket, have them tie on another piece of yarn and keep weaving.
- Encourage each child to keep weaving until reaching the top of the container.
- Have each child tuck the loose end of yarn underneath a few of the woven strands and then tie a knot to secure the loose end. Cut off any extra yarn.
- **Say:** You have made some beautiful baskets today.
- **Ask:** What are some things that baskets are used for?
- **Say:** In today's Bible story, we will hear about a basket being used for an unusual and special purpose.

Prepare

- ✓ Provide paper bowls, scissors, and yarn
- ✓ *Tip*: If you have younger children in your class, you may wish to precut some bowls.
- ✓ *Note*: The greater the number of cuts used, the more round the resulting basket will be.

Prepare

✓ Provide a large blanket.

✓ Recruit two volunteers to hold the blanket up to form a screen.

✓ *Tip*: If you have a large class, choose more than one child at a time to be the guesser and choose more than one child to hide each time.

Who Is Hiding?

• Choose one child to be the guesser.

• Have the guesser step to a part of the room where she or he cannot see the rest of the group.

• Choose one of the remaining children to hide behind the blanket. Have the remaining children switch places so it is not as obvious who is hiding.

• Invite the guesser to rejoin the group and try to guess who is hiding.

• When the child guesses correctly, have the missing child join the group.

• Choose another child to be the guesser and continue to play the game.

• **Say:** Hiding has been fun in this game. In today's Bible story, we will hear about a mother who needed to hide her baby for a serious and important reason.

Prepare

✓ Provide marbles, aluminum foil, trays for water, and towels.

✓ Fill the trays with water and set them on towels.

Floating Marbles

• Give each child a marble.

• **Ask:** What would happen if you placed your marble in the tray of water? (It would sink.)

• Let the children place the marbles in the water and watch them sink.

• **Ask:** How could you keep your marble from sinking?

• Allow children to share their ideas

• Give each child a square of aluminum foil.

• Encourage each child to use the foil to design a basket or boat that will support a marble when placed in water.

• Have the children test their foil baskets to see if they will float while holding a marble.

• If the trays are big enough, let the children blow their baskets across the water.

• **Say:** In today's Bible story, we will hear about a woman who needed to keep something important afloat.

Large Group

Bring all the children together to experience the Bible story. Use a bell to alert the children to the large-group time.

Who Am I Looking For?

- Have the children stand in a circle.
- **Say:** I am going to begin to describe someone in our circle. If I might be describing you, remain standing. If I am not describing you, sit down and try to guess who I am looking for.
- Choose a child and begin describing that child using sentences beginning with "I am looking for someone who…" For example, you might say, "I am looking for someone who is wearing blue. I am looking for someone who is wearing blue and has short hair. I am looking for someone who is wearing blue, has short hair, and has tennis shoes on."
- Continue describing the child until he or she is the only one standing.
- Have the children stand up again and play several more rounds as time permits.
- **Say:** As we hear our Bible story today, we will be looking for people who are doing God's work.

Moses' Story

- **Say:** Today we are beginning a six-week study about Moses. Moses was a prophet. A prophet is someone who delivers messages for God. The story of Moses' life is found in the second book of the Bible.
- **Ask:** What is the second book of the Bible? (Exodus)
- **Say:** Today we are going to hear the story of Moses' birth. We are going to hear the story as if Moses were telling it to us with the help of some friends.
- Invite your recruited volunteers to tell the story from **Reproducible 1a: The Birth of Moses.**
- Thank your volunteers for telling the story.
- **Ask:** Why was Moses' life in danger when he was born? (Pharaoh had made a law that all Israelite baby boys should be thrown in the Nile River.)
- **Say:** It was a scary time for the Israelites. They were slaves in Egypt and Pharaoh was trying to keep their population from growing.
- **Ask:** How do you think Moses' mother felt when she saw that her baby was a boy? (scared, worried)
- **Say:** Moses' mother did what she could to protect her baby. She was willing to let Pharaoh's daughter raise her son if it meant he would live.

Prepare

✓ Provide copies of **Reproducible 1a: The Birth of Moses**.

✓ Recruit a volunteer to come and read the story of Moses each week during this study. *Optional*: If Bible times costumes are available, have your volunteer dress as a shepherd.

✓ Invite several confident readers to help tell the Bible story. Give each reader a copy of the story. Encourage the readers to follow along as Moses tells the story. Have the readers read in unison the words that are in bold type.

The Birth of Moses

Prepare

✓ On a piece of mural paper or posterboard, write the heading "Four Courageous Women." Underneath the heading write: two midwives, Moses' mother, Pharaoh's daughter.

✓ Display the poster where the children will be able to see it.

Seeing God at Work

- **Say:** Today we heard the story of Moses' birth. When Moses grew up, he did several important jobs for God. He wouldn't have been able to do God's work if his life had not been saved when he was a baby. Four women acted bravely to keep Moses alive.

- Show the children the poster.

- **Ask:** What did the two midwives, Shiphrah and Puah, do to protect Moses and all Hebrew baby boys? (They refused to kill the Hebrew baby boys.)

- **Say:** Pharaoh asked the midwives to kill the Hebrew baby boys. Pharaoh was the most powerful man in Egypt. But the midwives knew that what he was asking them to do was wrong. They refused to follow Pharaoh's order. The midwives were brave and did the right thing.

- **Ask:** How did Moses' mother protect her baby? (She refused to throw him in the river. She hid him for three months. She put him in a basket on the river.)

- **Say:** Moses' mother took a chance to save her son. It was a brave thing to do. Technically she did put her baby in the river as Pharaoh had decreed, but she put him in a basket first.

- **Ask:** Who found baby Moses in his basket on the river? (Pharaoh's daughter) Do you think Pharaoh's daughter knew about her father's decree that all Hebrew baby boys were to be killed? (probably)

- **Say:** Like the midwives and Moses' mother, Pharaoh's daughter was brave too. She knew her father's law about Hebrew baby boys but she chose to save the baby's life.

- **Ask:** Do you think God was at work in this story to keep Moses alive? How do you see God at work in this story?

- Allow children an opportunity to share their thoughts.

- **Say:** God often works through the actions of people. We are God's hands and feet in the world. As we've seen, God worked through the actions of these four courageous women to protect Moses.

- Invite children to hold their hands up to their eyes and pretend they are looking through binoculars while you pray.

- **Pray:** God, thank you for stories of brave women doing your work. Help us to see the people around us that are doing your work. Help us to look for ways to share your love with other people. Amen.

Bible Verse Back and Forth

- Show the children today's Bible verse.

- **Say:** Today's Bible verse tells us how Moses got his name.

- Encourage the children to read the verse with you.

- **Ask:** Who is speaking in this verse? Who gave Moses his name? (Pharaoh's daughter)

- **Say:** In Hebrew, the word *Moses* sounds like the word that means "pull out."

- Divide the children into two groups.

- **Say:** Some of the words in this verse are spoken by Pharaoh's daughter, but not all of them.

- Assign one group to read the words spoken by Pharaoh's daughter. Have the other group play the role of the narrator and read the remaining words.

- Encourage the children to say the verse several times in the manner described.

- Dismiss children to their small groups.

Prepare

✓ Write this week's Bible verse on a markerboard or a piece of mural paper and place it where it can easily be seen. ("She named him Moses, 'because,' she said, 'I pulled him out of the water.'" Exodus 2:10b)

Small Groups

Divide the children into small groups. You may organize the groups around age levels or around readers and nonreaders. Keep the groups small, with a maximum of ten children in each group. You may need to have more than one group of each age level.

Young Children

- **Say:** We will be learning about Moses' life for six weeks. We are going to start making a big book about Moses. We will add to our book each week.

- Show the children the poster that says *Lessons from the Life of Moses.*

- **Say:** This will be the cover of our book.

- Encourage the children to work together to decorate the book cover.

- **Say:** Today we heard the story of the birth of Moses.

- **Ask:** Why was baby Moses' life in danger? (Pharaoh had ordered all Hebrew baby boys to be drowned.) Who did God's work and protected Moses? (the midwives, Moses' mother, and Pharaoh's daughter)

- Show the children the other posterboard.

- Encourage the children to work together to plan an illustration to go along with the words. One possibility is Moses' mother placing Moses in the river in a basket. Have the children draw the picture.

- Stack the two pieces of posterboard face up with the book cover lying on top.

- Tape the left edges of the posterboards together to form the beginning of a book.

- **Say:** The midwives, Moses' mother, and Pharaoh's daughter all did God's work and helped protect Moses. There are many ways to do God's work. Any time you help someone or show love to someone you are doing God's work.

- **Ask:** What are some ways you can do God's work?

- Allow children an opportunity to share their ideas.

- **Say:** This week look for ways you can do God's work.

- Save the big book to be used next week.

- **Pray:** God, thank you for stories that help us learn about you. Help us to do your work in the world. Amen.

Prepare

✓ Provide two pieces of posterboard, markers, crayons, and masking tape.

✓ Use a marker to write the following words in large block letters on one of the pieces of posterboard: *Lessons from the Life of Moses.*

✓ Use a marker to write the following words at the bottom of the other piece of posterboard, leaving room above the words for illustrations: "God works through people."

Older Children

- Have the children work together to tape the cardboard box shut and then cover the entire box with mural paper.

- **Say:** We will be learning about Moses' life for six weeks. We are going to use the box you have covered to make a cube to help us remember the lessons we learn as we hear about Moses' life.

- Have the children work together to write the words, *Lessons from the Life of Moses* on one side of the box. Let the children decorate this side of the box.

- **Ask:** Why was Moses' life in danger when he was born? (Pharaoh had decreed that all Hebrew baby boys should be killed.) Why was Pharaoh afraid the Israelites would take over Egypt? (There were so many of them.)

- **Say:** Earlier we discussed how God was at work early on in Moses' life through the actions of those around him.

- **Ask:** Who was doing God's work and protecting Moses? (the midwives, Moses' mother, Pharaoh's daughter)

- Have the children turn the box to a blank side and write the words, "God works though people." Let the children decorate this side of the box.

- **Say:** There are many ways to do God's work.

- **Ask:** What are some ways you can do God's work? How does it make you feel to know God is working through you?

- Allow children an opportunity to share their ideas.

- **Say:** One way we can do God's work is to pray for other people.

- **Ask:** Whom would you like to pray for today?

- Invite children to share prayer concerns.

- **Pray:** God, we lift the people we have named up to you as well as those we name silently. Help us to look for ways to do your work in the world. Amen.

- Save the story cube to be used next week.

Prepare

✓ Provide a square cardboard box, mural paper, tape, scissors, markers, and crayons.

✓ *Tip*: Any size cardboard box can be used. Make sure the box is large enough to allow space for writing.

The Birth of Moses

Hello! My name is Moses. Today I want to tell you about something that happened shortly after I was born. At the time of my birth, my people, who were known as the Israelites, or the Hebrews, were slaves in Egypt.

This doesn't sound good for the Israelites.

It wasn't good. The ruler of Egypt, who was known as Pharaoh, forced the Israelites to make mortar and bricks, work in the fields, and do other hard labor for the Egyptians. Even while they were working as slaves, the numbers of the Israelites continued to grow. Pharaoh became worried that the Israelites would take over Egypt. He decided to use his power to keep this from happening.

Uh-oh. What did he do?

Pharaoh talked to two midwives named Shiphrah and Puah. Midwives helped pregnant women when it was time for their babies to be born. Pharaoh told the midwives that when they delivered a Hebrew baby boy they were to kill it. Hebrew baby girls were allowed to live.

That's terrible!

Well, Shiphrah and Puah thought it was terrible too. They refused to kill the Hebrew babies. Pharaoh called for the midwives and asked them why they were letting the baby boys live.

What did they say?

They told him that the Hebrew women were so strong they were giving birth without the help of the midwives. These two women were brave when speaking to Pharaoh.

Good for the midwives!

Pharaoh was determined to keep the Israelite population from growing. He ordered that all baby boys born to the Hebrews should be thrown into the Nile River where they would drown.

That's horrible!

It was a scary time for the Israelites. But one mother found a way to save her son.

How did she do that?

This Hebrew woman gave birth to a boy. At first she was able to hide him from the Egyptians. When the baby was three months old, she realized she would no longer be able to hide him. So she made a basket and covered the inside of the basket with tar so it would be waterproof. She put the baby in the basket and placed that basket among the reeds in the river. The baby's sister watched to see what would happen.

What happened?

The daughter of Pharaoh was walking by the river and found the baby in the basket.

What did she do?

Pharaoh's daughter recognized the baby was a Hebrew and she felt sorry for him. The baby's sister appeared and offered to find a Hebrew woman to take care of the baby. When Pharaoh's daughter agreed, she went and got their mother. Pharaoh's daughter asked the woman to care for the baby until it was old enough to come and live with her at the palace.

So the baby's mother was able to keep him after all?

Yes, the baby's mother took care of him until he was old enough to go and live with Pharaoh's daughter. Then Pharaoh's daughter adopted him and named him Moses.

Based on Exodus 1:8–2:10

2. The Burning Bush

Objectives

The children will:

- hear the story of God calling Moses.
- discover that Moses heard God's call because he was paying attention.
- explore ways to pay attention to God calling them.

Bible Story

The Burning Bush
Exodus 2:11–3:22

Bible Verse

"So get going. I'm sending you to Pharaoh to bring my people, the Israelites, out of Egypt."

Exodus 3:10

Focus for the Teacher

As we continue our study of Moses, the reluctant prophet, this week we will hear the story of the call of Moses. God called Moses in a dramatic way, by speaking from a burning bush. Moses could have walked on by the burning bush and missed God's call, but instead he was paying attention and chose to investigate. To hear God's call in our lives, we need to pay attention.

Moses was surprised God was choosing him. Moses' response to God's call was typical of the way many of us respond when we feel God is asking us to do something. He began making excuses. "Who am I to go to Pharaoh and to bring the Israelites out of Egypt?" he asked God (Exodus 3:11). After all, Moses had fled Egypt because he had killed an Egyptian. Yet God chose him for an important job. There was no doubt this call was meant for Moses—the voice from the burning bush called him by name. This was not a mistake. Sometimes we may feel surprised God is choosing us. Whatever our past experiences, God can use us to do God's work.

> To hear God's call in our lives, we need to pay attention.

To reassure Moses, God promised him he would not be alone. Out of the flames of the bush came a reassuring promise, "I'll be with you." Just as God was with Moses, God is with us in whatever God calls us to do.

Most of us have not experienced God speaking to us from a burning bush. That doesn't mean God doesn't have a plan for us. God's message for us today tends to be delivered in subtler ways.

Help your children understand that God still communicates with us today, though in a different way than God spoke to Moses. We hear God's voice when we help someone in need and when we love and care for others.

Explore Interest Groups

Be sure that adult leaders are waiting when the first child arrives. Greet and welcome each child. Get the children involved in an activity that interests them and introduces the theme for the day's activities.

Paint a Burning Bush

- Give each child a piece of paper.
- **Say:** In today's Bible story, we will hear about a bush. Right now I would like you to draw a bush on your paper.
- Invite each child to use crayons to draw a bush. Encourage children to draw branches and add leaves. Have the children press firmly with the crayons.
- **Say:** The bush we will hear about in the Bible story was on fire, but it was not being destroyed by the flames.
- **Say:** You are going to use watercolor paints to add flames to your bush. The crayon will resist the paint and show through even if you paint over it.
- Show the children how to use the watercolor paints by dipping a paintbrush in water, mixing it with the paint and then painting on the paper.
- Encourage children to use red, orange, and yellow watercolor paints to add flames to their bushes.
- Set the pictures aside to dry.

Prepare

- ✓ Provide paper, crayons, watercolor paints, paintbrushes, plastic containers for water, and plastic or paper table coverings.
- ✓ Protect the work area with plastic or paper.
- ✓ Fill plastic containers one-third full with water and place them in the center of the table with the watercolor paints.
- ✓ *Option*: Some children may enjoy using their handprint to draw the bush. Have children use a crayon to trace around one of their hands with the fingers spread apart. Encourage children to color in the handprint and then add leaves to the branches represented by their fingers.

God's Name

- Give each child a copy of **Reproducible 2a: God's Name** and a pencil.
- Encourage each child to complete the puzzle.
- Have the children look up Exodus 3:14 to check their answers.

Prepare

- ✓ Provide copies of **Reproducible 2a: God's Name**.
- ✓ Supply Bibles and pencils.
- ✓ *Answer*: God said to Moses, "I Am Who I Am."

Prepare

✓ Provide paper cups, string, paper clips, scissors, and sharp pencils.

Can You Hear Your Name?

- Have each child find a partner.
- Give each pair of children two paper cups and two paper clips.
- Encourage the children to follow these directions to make a paper cup telephone:
  o Use a sharp pencil to poke a small hole in the bottom of each cup.
  o Cut a piece of string that is almost long enough to reach from one side of the room to the other.
  o Thread each end of the string through the bottom of a paper cup so the end of the string is inside the cup.
  o Tie a paper clip to each end of the string.
- Have each child hold one of the paper cups and have the children walk away from each other until the string is pulled tight.
- Encourage one child to hold the cup to his or her ear.
- Have the other child hold the cup to his or her mouth, and say the other child's name two times.
- Encourage the children to take turns listening and speaking.
- Have the children speak to each other across the room without the use of the paper cup telephone and compare how well they can hear each other with and without the phone.
- Challenge the children to experiment with the following changes to see how the delivery of sound is affected:
  o Do not pull the string tight.
  o Have a third person hold on to the middle of the string.
- **Say:** In today's Bible story, we will hear about God calling Moses' name. However, God didn't use a paper cup telephone to get Moses' attention.

Who Is Calling?

- Have the children sit in a circle.
- Call one child by name and invite that child to sit in the center of the circle and close his or her eyes.
- Tap another child on the shoulder and have that child call out the name of the child in the center two times.
- Have the child in the center open his or her eyes and guess the identity of the speaker.
- If the guess is correct, have the children change places.
- If the guess is incorrect, the child in the middle stays and and closes his or her eyes again.
- **Say:** In today's Bible story, we will hear about a time Moses heard someone calling his name.

Large Group

Bring all the children together to experience the Bible story. Use a bell to alert the children to the large-group time.

Take Off Your Shoes

- Have the children stand in a circle.
- Invite the children to take off their shoes and place them in the middle of the circle.
- **Say:** The reason we have taken our shoes off is related to the Bible story. We will leave our shoes off as we hear the story. As you listen to the story, pay attention to figure out why we've removed our shoes.
- Encourage the children to move to the story area and sit down.
- Leave the shoes where they are until later in the lesson.

Moses' Story

- **Say:** Last week we heard the story of Moses' birth. When he was born, Moses' life was in danger because of Pharaoh's decree that all Hebrew baby boys should be killed.
- **Ask:** Who protected Moses? What actions did they take to protect Moses? (The two midwives refused to kill the Hebrew babies. Moses' mother hid him and then put him in a basket on the Nile River. Pharaoh's daughter found Moses and adopted him.)
- **Say:** Today we are continuing to hear Moses' story. The story of Moses is found in Exodus, the second book of the Bible. We are going to hear the story as if Moses were telling it to us with the help of some friends.
- Invite your recruited volunteers to tell the story from **Reproducible 2b: The Burning Bush.**
- Thank your volunteers for telling the story.
- **Ask:** Why did we take our shoes off today? What do you think holy ground is?
- Allow children an opportunity to share their thoughts.
- **Ask:** How do you think Moses felt when he realized God was speaking to him out of the burning bush? Why do you think God chose a burning bush to speak to Moses? What do you think would have happened if Moses hadn't been paying attention and had walked on by the bush?
- Allow children an opportunity to share their ideas.
- **Say:** Moses was paying attention and he noticed the burning bush. Although he was at first reluctant to do what God asked, he eventually agreed.

Prepare

✓ Provide copies of **Reproducible 2b: The Burning Bush**.

✓ Recruit a volunteer to come and read the story of Moses each week. *Optional*: If Bible times costumes are available, have your volunteer dress as a shepherd.

✓ Invite several confident readers to help tell the Bible story. Give each reader a copy of the story. Encourage the readers to follow along as Moses tells the story. Have the readers read the words in bold type in unison.

Prepare

✓ Write this week's Bible verse on a markerboard or a piece of mural paper and place it where it can easily be seen. ("So get going. I'm sending you to Pharaoh to bring my people, the Israelites, out of Egypt." Exodus 3:10)

Voice of God Bible Verse

- Show the children today's Bible verse.
- Encourage the children to read the verse with you.
- **Ask:** Who is speaking the words in this verse? (God) Who was God speaking to? (Moses)
- **Say:** We don't know what God's voice sounds like. Let's use our imaginations to think about what God's voice might sound like.
- Invite a child to choose a type of voice such as loud, soft, squeaky, slow, bouncy, and so forth.
- Have the class say the verse together using the chosen type of voice.
- Give other children an opportunity to choose a type of voice for the class to use as the Bible verse is read.

God Is Calling Us

- Invite the children to sit in a circle around their shoes.
- **Say:** Earlier we took off our shoes just as Moses took off his shoes when God called to him from a burning bush. We did this as a reminder that this space is holy ground.
- **Ask:** Has God ever spoken to you from a burning bush?
- **Say:** Most of us have never experienced God speaking to us from a burning bush. However, we can still hear God speaking to us. God may not speak to us in a voice we can hear like God spoke to Moses, but when we pay attention we may hear God speaking to us through the world around us. God may speak to us through the voice of a friend or the words in the Bible or the feeling we get when we are outside in God's world.
- **Ask:** What are some other ways God may send us messages?
- Allow children an opportunity to share their ideas.
- **Say:** If Moses hadn't been paying attention, he might have missed the burning bush. This is true for us too. We need to pay attention in order to see when God is asking us to do something. God asked Moses to lead the Israelites from slavery in Egypt. Obviously, that's not what God is asking us to do, but there are many other ways we can do God's work.
- **Ask:** What are some things God might ask us to do?
- Allow children an opportunity to share their thoughts.
- **Say:** When God told Moses what he was to do, Moses was reluctant. God promised to be with Moses and eventually Moses agreed to do as God asked. No matter what God is calling us to do, we know God will be with us. Our response can be "Here I am, send me." I am going to pick up a pair of shoes. If the shoes belong to you, say, "Here I am, send me," and come and get your shoes.
- Pick up one pair of shoes at a time, encouraging each child to respond, until all the children have retrieved their shoes.
- **Pray:** God, here we are, ready to do your work. Help us to pay attention so that when you call us, we will get the message. Amen.
- Dismiss children to their small groups.

Moses: Children's Leader Guide

Small Groups

Divide the children into small groups. You may organize the groups around age levels or around readers and nonreaders. Keep the groups small, with a maximum of ten children in each group. You may need to have more than one group of each age level.

Young Children

- **Say:** Last week we began making a big book.
- Show the children the book *Lessons from the Life of Moses*.
- Turn to the first page of the book.
- **Say:** Last week we heard the story of courageous women who protected Moses when he was a baby.
- **Ask:** What lesson did we learn from that story? (God works through people.)
- **Say:** God was at work through the actions of the women in Moses' life and God also works through our actions. This week we heard the story of God calling Moses. God also calls us to do God's work. We have talked about ways God might be calling us. Our lesson for this week is that we need to pay attention.
- Show the children the posterboard you have prepared.
- Encourage the children to work together to plan an illustration to go along with the words. One possibility is Moses and the burning bush. Have the children draw the picture.
- Tape the new piece of posterboard onto the back of the book.
- **Say:** God calls us to do God's work wherever we are.
- **Ask:** What are some ways to do God's work at home? What are some ways to do God's work at church? What are some ways to do God's work at school?
- Invite children to share their ideas.
- **Say:** You have great ideas about ways to do God's work. Remember to pay attention, so you know what God wants you to do.
- **Pray:** God, thank you for stories that remind us you have a job for us to do. Help us to look for ways to share your love with other people. Amen.
- Save the big book to be used next week.

Prepare

✓ Provide a piece of posterboard, markers, crayons, and masking tape.

✓ Supply the big book of *Lessons from the Life of Moses* started last week.

✓ Use a marker to write the following words at the bottom of a piece of posterboard, leaving room above the words for illustrations: "Pay attention—God is calling!"

Prepare

✓ Provide markers and crayons.

✓ Supply the story cube started last week.

Older Children

- Show the children the side of the story cube that says, *Lessons from the Life of Moses*.

- **Say:** Last week we began making a cube to help us review the lessons we learn as we are talking about Moses' life.

- Show the children the side of the story cube that says, "God works through people."

- **Say:** Last week we heard the story of Moses as a baby and we learned that God works through people.

- **Ask:** What people did God's work to protect Moses when he was a baby? (the midwives, Moses' mother, Pharaoh's daughter)

- **Say:** This week we heard the story of God calling Moses. God also calls us to do God's work. We have talked about ways God might be calling us. Our lesson for this week is that we need to pay attention.

- Have the children turn to a blank side of the cube and write the words, "Pay attention—God is calling!" Let the children decorate this side of the box.

- **Say:** God called to Moses from a burning bush while he was out in the field watching his father-in-law's sheep. God can call us wherever we are. There are opportunities to do God's work everywhere.

- **Ask:** What opportunities are there to do God's work when you are at home? What opportunities are there to do God's work at church? What opportunities are there to do God's work at school?

- Allow children an opportunity to share their ideas.

- **Ask:** What are some ways we might figure out what God wants us to do? (pray, read the Bible, go to church, talk to other people, spend time in nature, listen)

- **Say:** Remember to pay attention so you notice when God is calling you to do something.

- **Pray:** God, it's not always easy to know what you want us to do. Help us to pay attention so we can recognize your voice. We are willing to do your work. Amen.

- Save the story cube to be used next week.

God's Name

God asked Moses to go to Egypt and tell Pharaoh to free the Israelites from slavery. Moses wanted to know how the Israelites would know that God sent him. Moses said to God, "When they ask me, What is this God's name, what am I supposed to tell them?"

T O A D S   H O W   A I M   G O O S E S   M I D   A I M

That's not what God said! All the letters are there, but they are in the wrong order. Number the letters in the above sentence. Then write each letter in the correct space below to find out God's reply to Moses.

_____   _____   _____   _____

12-2-20   17-9-19-4   1-7   23-13-5-16-15

_____   _____   _____   _____   _____

10   21-11   8-6-14   22   3-18

The Burning Bush

Hello! My name is Moses. Last week I told you about my mother putting me in a basket on the river when I was a baby. Pharaoh's daughter found me and took me to the palace to live. Today I want to tell you about something that happened after I had grown up. My people, the Israelites, were still slaves in Egypt. I wasn't living in Egypt anymore.

Why did you leave Egypt?

I had to leave Egypt after I grew up because one day I got angry and did something I shouldn't have done. When Pharaoh heard what I had done, he wanted to kill me, so I left Egypt and went to a place called Midian.

What did you do there?

In Midian, I made a new home, got married, and had a son. After many years had passed, one day I was out taking care of my father-in-law's sheep. As I was walking around I noticed the strangest thing. I saw a bush that was on fire. It was the strangest thing—even though the bush was on fire, it wasn't burning up!

What did you do?

I was curious and decided to investigate. As I came close to the bush, I heard my name, "Moses, Moses!" You can imagine my surprise at hearing a burning bush call my name! Then the voice from the bush told me to take off my shoes because I was standing on holy ground. The voice went on to tell me it was God talking to me—the God of my father, the God of Abraham, Isaac, and Jacob. By this time I was so afraid I hid my face.

What else did God say?

From the burning bush, God told me the Israelites were still slaves in Egypt and God had heard their cries of suffering. God said, "So get going. I'm sending you to Pharaoh to bring my people, the Israelites, out of Egypt."

Why did God choose you?

That's what I asked. I couldn't believe my ears! "Who am I that I should go to Pharaoh and lead your people out of Egypt?" I asked. "Why are you asking me to do this?"

God said, "I will go with you. You won't be alone."

Did you go?

I still wasn't sure I was the right person for the job, but I felt better knowing I wouldn't be alone. God chose me to lead the Israelites out of Egypt and God promised to be with me. When God asks you to do something, you do it.

What happened next?

That's a story for another day.

Based on Exodus 2:11–3:22

3. The Exodus

Objectives

The children will:

- hear the story of God freeing the Israelites from slavery in Egypt.

- discover that God was at work through Moses to free the Israelites.

- explore what it means to be claimed as God's people.

Bible Story

The Exodus
Exodus 5:1-2; 6:1-10; 12:31–14:31

Bible Verse

"I'll take you as my people, and I'll be your God."

Exodus 6:7a

Focus for the Teacher

Last week we heard about God calling Moses for a special task: to go to Egypt and tell Pharaoh to free the Israelites from slavery. In this week's Bible story, Moses is on the job with his brother, Aaron. When Moses was making excuses to try and avoid God's call, he told God he'd never been any good at speaking. God's solution was to have Moses take Aaron with him to do the talking.

Moses and Aaron approached Pharaoh and asked him to let the Israelite people go. In order to convince Pharaoh to release the Israelites from slavery, God performed a series of powerful acts. The plagues were designed to change Pharaoh's mind, but also to display God's power and demonstrate God's control over all of creation. This pattern was repeated until God sends death to the Egyptians and Pharaoh finally agreed to let them go.

After years of slavery in Egypt, the Israelites were finally free. It would seem like this would be a wonderful thing. Yet at one point the Israelites cried out to Moses, "What have you done to us, bringing us out of Egypt?" (Exodus 14:11). The Israelites were afraid. They were leaving a life of slavery, but it was the life they knew. They were leaving for an unknown land

> God has claimed us as God's people.

and a new way of life. It turns out that leaving Egypt was the beginning of a long struggle for freedom. As they left Egypt, Pharaoh's army began to follow them. Pharaoh had changed his mind (again) after the Israelites left. He may have realized what the loss of his slave workforce would mean. Pursued by Pharaoh's army and facing an uncertain future, the Israelites began to question whether God was really with them. Moses once again reminded them to trust God. God had claimed the Israelites as God's people. God had brought them this far, and God would deliver them from the Egyptians.

Sometimes we may act like the Israelites and question whether God is really with us. When we are scared and feeling overwhelmed by life, we may wonder where God is in the midst of our turmoil. Just as the Israelites could see no way out, sometimes we may feel trapped by life's circumstances. At these times it is good to remember that, like the Israelites, God has claimed us as God's people. Moses reminded the Israelites to put their trust in God. God provided a way for the Israelites by parting the waters of the Reed Sea so the Israelites could cross. God provided a path to freedom.

Explore Interest Groups

Be sure that adult leaders are waiting when the first child arrives. Greet and welcome each child. Get the children involved in an activity that interests them and introduces the theme for the day's activities.

Walk Through Paper

- Hold up a sheet of paper.

- **Ask:** Do you think I can walk through this piece of paper? Do you think our entire class would fit through this piece of paper?

- Give each child a piece of paper and a pair of scissors.

- Have each child fold his or her paper in half lengthwise, bringing the long edges together.

- Show the children how to cut the paper.
  - o   Have each child begin cutting on the folded edge near one end of the paper and cut through almost to the other side.
  - o   Have each child cut a line parallel to the first cut, but beginning at the non-folded edge of the paper, again stopping before she or he reaches the edge.
  - o   Encourage each child to continue cutting parallel lines, alternating starting the cuts on the folded and non-folded edges of the paper. The last cut should begin on the folded edge.
  - o   Have each child lay his or her paper flat on the table, still folded.
  - o   Show each child how to cut along the fold on every strip except the first and last strip.

- Have each child open up the paper, which will now be a large circle that he or she can easily walk through.

- Challenge the children to see if they can cut a piece of paper your entire class can fit in. The closer together the cuts are made, the larger the circle will be.

- Lay the resulting circle on the floor and see if everyone can stand inside the paper circle.

- **Say**: It sounds unbelievable to say you can walk through a piece of paper, but it's possible. In our Bible story today we will hear about a time God showed the Israelites a way to walk through water.

Prepare
- ✓ Provide paper and scissors.
- ✓ *Tip*: For young children, draw lines on the paper as a cutting guide.

Prepare

Science Fun

- Divide the children into groups of up to six children each.

- Give each group of children a tray of water.

- Have the children sprinkle pepper on top of the water. Encourage the children to sprinkle enough pepper to cover the surface of the water.

- Invite the children to stick a bar of soap in the water in the middle of the pepper.

- **Ask:** What happened to the pepper when you put the soap in the water? (It moved away from the soap.)

- Have the children remove the bar of soap and sprinkle sugar in the empty area where there is now no pepper.

- **Ask:** What happened to the pepper when you sprinkled sugar in the water? (The pepper moved back together.)

- **Say:** When you add soap to the water it interferes with the surface tension of the water, causing the pepper to be pushed away. The addition of sugar restores the surface tension properties of the water.

- Let the children experiment with the pepper and the soap, placing the soap at the edge of the tray and in the middle.

- **Say:** In this experiment it is pepper that is being separated in the water. In our Bible story today we will hear about a time when water itself was separated.

Prepare

✓ Identify a large open area to play the game.

Let Us Go, Pharaoh!

- **Say:** Last week we heard about God calling Moses to do a special job. Moses was to go to Egypt and tell Pharaoh to free the Israelites from slavery. We are going to play a game called, "Let us go, Pharaoh!"

- Choose a child to be Pharaoh.

- **Say:** The rest of you are Israelites. You want to be free.

- Have all children, including Pharaoh, stand on one side of the room, facing the other side of the room.

- **Say:** All of you except Pharaoh will say together, "Let us go, Pharaoh!" Pharaoh will say, "Okay, you may take two steps," or whatever number he or she chooses. You will each then count off the number of steps Pharaoh has given permission to move. Then you will ask the question again. Pharaoh will respond again and you will move again. At some point, Pharaoh, instead of giving a number will say, "I changed my mind!" That is your cue to run to the other side of the room. Pharaoh will chase you and tag someone to be the new Pharaoh.

- Encourage the children to play the game.

Large Group

Bring all the children together to experience the Bible story. Use a bell to alert the children to the large-group time.

An Exodus

- Invite the children to gather in the spot you have selected.
- **Say:** We have been hearing stories of Moses' life. These stories are found in the second book of the Bible.
- **Ask:** What is the second book of the Bible? (Exodus)
- **Say:** The Book of Exodus is named for the story we are going to hear from Moses today.
- **Ask:** What does the word *exodus* mean?
- **Say:** The word *exodus* means a mass exit. It refers to a lot of people leaving at one time. In our Bible story Exodus refers to the Israelite people leaving Egypt where they had been slaves for over four hundred years. Right now we are going to have an exodus to our story area.
- Invite the children to move to your story area.

Prepare

✓ Select a spot for the children to gather that is separate from your story area.

Moses' Story

- **Say:** God spoke to Moses from a burning bush and asked him to do an important job. We are continuing to hear the story of Moses from Moses' viewpoint.
- Invite your recruited volunteers to tell the story from **Reproducible 3a: The Exodus.**
- Thank your volunteers for telling the story.
- **Ask:** Was Pharaoh happy to let the Israelites go? Why do you think Pharaoh didn't want the Israelites to leave? (They were his slaves. They did a lot of work in Egypt.)
- **Say:** The Israelites were slaves in Egypt for over four hundred years. Life in slavery was hard and they were not happy. God heard the people's cry for help and sent Moses to lead them out of slavery.
- **Ask:** How do you think the Israelites were feeling as they left Egypt?
- Allow children an opportunity to share their thoughts.
- **Say:** Although they were leaving a life of slavery, the Israelites soon found out that there were still challenges to be faced.
- **Ask:** How do you think the Israelites felt when they realized Pharaoh's army was chasing them?
- Allow children an opportunity to share their ideas.
- **Say:** Moses had to remind the Israelites to trust God. This is an important thing to remember.

Prepare

✓ Provide copies of **Reproducible 3a: The Exodus**.

✓ Recruit a volunteer to come and read the story of Moses each week. *Optional*: If Bible times costumes are available, have your volunteer dress as a shepherd.

✓ Invite several confident readers to help tell the Bible story. Give each reader a copy of the story. Encourage the readers to follow along as Moses tells the story. Have the readers read the words in bold type in unison.

Prepare

✓ Write this week's Bible verse on a markerboard or a piece of mural paper and place it where it can easily be seen. ("I'll take you as my people, and I'll be your God." Exodus 6:7a)

Prepare

✓ Place a blue sheet on the floor in a place where the children can gather around it in a circle.

✓ *Optional*: If you do not have a blue sheet, place pieces of blue construction paper on the floor.

Clap and Stomp the Bible Verse

- Show the children the Bible verse poster.
- Encourage the children to read the verse with you.
- **Ask:** Who is speaking in this verse? (God)
- **Say:** This is God's reminder to the Israelites that God has chosen them. God has chosen us to be God's people too. Let's read the verse again. This time as we read the verse we will clap as we say each word.
- Invite the children to read the verse with you, clapping as directed.
- **Say:** This time as we read the verse we will stomp our foot as we say each word.
- Have the children read the verse as directed.
- **Say:** We are going to read the verse again. This time for a challenge we will clap on the first word and stomp our foot on the second word. We'll alternate clapping and stomping with each word.
- Encourage the children to read the verse again, clapping and stomping as directed.

We Are God's People

- Invite the children to sit in a circle around the blue sheet.
- **Say:** In today's Bible story, Moses led the Israelites out of Egypt, but their worries were not over.
- **Ask:** What were the Israelites worried about in today's story? (Pharaoh's army was chasing them.)
- **Say:** Moses reminded the Israelites to trust God. He reminded them that God had chosen them to be God's people.
- **Ask:** What does it mean to be God's people?
- Allow children an opportunity to share their thoughts.
- **Say:** The Israelites didn't know where they were going or how they were going to escape from the Egyptians. Moses helped them by reminding them to trust God. Trusting in God doesn't mean we won't be scared, or we won't ever have things that worry us. But as God's people we are never alone because God is always with us.
- **Ask:** How does it make you feel to know God is always with you?
- **Say:** We are going to pretend this blue sheet is the sea and we are going to imagine tossing the things that worry us into the sea.
- Have children think of something that worries them or makes them sad.
- Encourage children to cup their hands near their mouths and whisper their worries into their hands.
- Invite children to imagine holding their worries in their hands and then to pretend to throw them into the sea as they say out loud, "I trust God!"
- **Pray:** God, thank you for choosing us to be your people. We are giving you the things we are worried about and trusting you. Amen.
- Dismiss children to their small groups.

Moses: Children's Leader Guide

Small Groups

Divide the children into small groups. You may organize the groups around age levels or around readers and nonreaders. Keep the groups small, with a maximum of ten children in each group. You may need to have more than one group of each age level.

Young Children

- **Say:** As we learn about Moses' life, we have been making a big book.

- Show children the book *Lessons from the Life of Moses*.

- Read the book together, encouraging the children to tell you what they remember about the stories of baby Moses and the burning bush.

- Show the children the posterboard you have prepared for this week.

- Encourage the children to work together to plan an illustration to go along with the words. One possibility is the parting of the Reed Sea. Have the children draw the picture.

- Tape the new piece of posterboard onto the back of the book.

- **Say:** When the Israelites were freed from slavery, they had to learn to trust God. It wasn't always easy for them to remember that God would always be with them. Moses helped the Israelites remember to trust God.

- **Ask:** Who helps you remember God's presence? Who helps you remember to trust God?

- **Say:** As we pray today let's thank God for choosing us to be God's people and let's thank God for the people in our lives that remind us to trust God.

- **Pray:** God, thank you for loving us and choosing us to be your children. Thank you for the people we have named that help us to remember your presence with us always. We love you and trust you. Amen.

- Save the big book to be used next week.

Prepare

- ✓ Provide a piece of posterboard, markers, crayons, and masking tape.

- ✓ Supply the big book of *Lessons from the Life of Moses* started two weeks ago.

- ✓ Use a marker to write the following words at the bottom of a piece of posterboard, leaving room above the words for illustrations: "We are God's people. We can trust God!"

Prepare

✓ Provide markers and crayons.

✓ Supply the story cube started two weeks ago.

Older Children

- **Say:** As we have been hearing Moses' story, we have been making a story cube to remind us of the lessons we've been learning.

- Encourage the children to look at the story and review the stories of baby Moses and the burning bush.

- **Ask:** What part of Moses' story did we hear today?

- Encourage children to work together to review today's Bible story.

- Have the children turn to a blank side of the cube and write the words, "We are God's people. We can trust God!" Let the children decorate this side of the box.

- **Say:** The Israelites weren't used to trusting in God. Moses had to remind them God had chosen them to be God's people.

- **Ask:** What does it mean to trust in God? Does trusting in God mean that everything in your life will be easy? How does trusting in God make your life different?

- Invite children to share their thoughts and ideas.

- **Say:** Trusting in God doesn't mean that we will never face challenges. God promises to be with us in whatever we face in life. Moses reminded the Israelites God was with them.

- **Ask:** Who reminds you of God's presence?

- **Pray:** God, thank you for claiming us as your people. Help us to remember to trust you and know you will be with us through everything we face in life. Amen.

- Save the story cube to be used next week.

The Exodus

Hello again! Moses here, back to tell you another story. Last week I told you about God calling to me from a burning bush. God asked me to lead the Israelites out of Egypt where they had been in slavery for over four hundred years. As God had asked, I went to Egypt and told Pharaoh to let the Israelites leave.

What did Pharaoh say?

As you can imagine, it wasn't easy to convince Pharaoh to let the Israelites go. It took many powerful acts of God before Pharaoh was convinced. Several times Pharaoh agreed to let us go and then he changed his mind. Finally, Pharaoh agreed and told me that the Israelites could leave.

Where did you go?

When we left Egypt, God showed us where we were to go by providing a pillar of cloud and fire for us to follow. During the day the pillar of cloud led us. At night a pillar of fire showed us which way to go. We were headed toward Canaan, the land God had promised us.

Nice to be done with Pharaoh!

Well, not quite. After we left Egypt, Pharaoh changed his mind again and decided he didn't want to let the Israelites go. I think he realized all of his slaves were gone. Pharaoh sent his army after us. The war chariots were very fast, and since we were traveling on foot, they were able to catch up with us. Soon we came to the Reed Sea. The Reed Sea was in front of us and Pharaoh's army was behind us.

Uh-oh. That's not good!

No, it wasn't. The people began to panic and ask me, "Why did you bring us out of Egypt? Did you bring us into the wilderness so we could die here instead of in Egypt?" They were scared, and I understood. It was frightening to see Pharaoh's army following us. Since I had led them out of Egypt, they looked to me for reassurance.

What did you tell the people?

When God asked me to lead the Israelites out of Egypt, God had promised to always be with me. I knew we could trust God. I reminded the Israelites of the message God had me deliver to them while they were still in Egypt, "I will take you as my people and I will be your God." I encouraged the people to continue to trust in God.

What happened?

Even as I was encouraging everyone else to trust in God, I wasn't sure how God was going to help us this time. It felt like we were trapped between Pharaoh's army and the Reed Sea. God told me to hold my walking stick over the sea. When I did, God parted the water so we could cross on dry land. It was amazing! The Egyptian army continued to follow us, but their chariot wheels got stuck and they started to panic. Then God made the water come back and the entire Egyptian army was tossed into the sea. We trusted in God and God delivered us from the Egyptians.

Based on Exodus 5:1-2; 6:1-10; 12:31–14:31

4. The Ten Commandments

<table>
<tr><td>

Objectives

The children will:

- hear the story of God giving the Israelites the Ten Commandments.
- discover that God gives us rules to help us know how to live.
- explore what it means to live by God's rules.

</td><td>

Bible Story

The Ten Commandments
Exodus 19:1–20:21

Bible Verse

"I am the LORD your God."
Exodus 20:2a

</td></tr>
</table>

Focus for the Teacher

The longest psalm in the Bible, Psalm 119, is a song of praise about God's laws. At one point, the psalmist exclaims, "But I love your commandments more than gold, /even more than pure gold" (Psalm 119:127). Few of us adore laws and rules enough to write a 176-verse psalm about them. We can, however, see the point the psalmist is trying to make. In general, rules are a good thing. Laws and rules provide structure for our lives. They provide a framework within which we can know how we are to act. God's laws help us know how to love and serve God and how to live in relationship with each other.

The first and probably most famous set of God's laws given to the Israelites following their escape from slavery in Egypt are the Ten Commandments. Even though it has been over three thousand years since God gave the Ten Commandments to the Israelites, these basic laws about relating to God and to other people are still applicable to our lives today.

The Ten Commandments are more than a list of dos and don'ts. These laws are about our relationships with God and others. Four of

> These rules are about our relationships with God and others.

the commandments address the relationship between God and us as God's chosen people. Because we are chosen as God's people, we are to be loyal to God alone. We are not to worship anyone or anything except God and we are to honor God's name. Being in relationship with God includes setting aside a day to rest and worship God.

The remaining six commandments address our relationship with one another. To live together in community, we need to treat each other with love and respect. These commandments provide a framework for living together as God's people.

Children are used to rules. They have rules to follow at home, at school, and even at church. Children may sometimes express frustration with following the rules imposed on them by others. The Ten Commandments may seem like just another set of rules designed to make their lives difficult! Help your children understand God does not give us commandments to make our lives harder, but to help us know how to live. If we trust in God's rules, they can help us live full and joyful lives.

Explore Interest Groups

Be sure that adult leaders are waiting when the first child arrives. Greet and welcome each child. Get the children involved in an activity that interests them and introduces the theme for the day's activities.

Rules, Rules, Rules

- Lay the prepared mural paper out on a table or on the floor where the children will be able to write on it.

- Encourage the children to think about rules they have to follow when they are at home, at school, and at church.

- Invite the children to write the rules on the corresponding section of the paper.

- Encourage the children to think of as many rules as they can.

- Assist younger children who may need help with writing.

- **Say:** It seems like there are a lot of rules.

- **Ask:** Are there some rules that are the same no matter where you are?

- **Say:** Today's Bible story will tell us about God's rules.

Prepare

- ✓ Provide mural paper, scissors, and markers.

- ✓ Cut a large sheet of mural paper. Divide the sheet into three sections. At the top of each section, write one of the following headings: "Rules at Home," "Rules at School," "Rules at Church."

Sculpture of Ten

- Invite each child to choose ten strips of construction paper.

- **Say:** Today we are going to hear about Ten Commandments. Right now you are going to use your ten strips of paper to make a sculpture.

- Give each child a piece of cardstock to use as a base for their sculpture.

- **Say:** The cardstock will be the base for your structure. Your building supplies are the ten paper strips you have chosen. You may fold or curl the paper strips to create your sculpture. You may use glue or staplers to attach the strips to your cardstock base or to each other.

- Invite each child to create a sculpture.

- Affirm each child's work.

- Encourage the children to admire each other's artwork.

Prepare

- ✓ Provide cardstock, construction paper, glue sticks, staplers, and tape.

- ✓ Use a paper cutter or scissors to cut the construction paper into 1-inch by 12-inch strips.

Prepare

✓ Provide paper and pencils.

Ten New Words

- Give each child a piece of paper and a pencil.

- Encourage each child to write the words *Ten Commandments* at the top of the paper.

- Challenge each child to use the letters in the words *Ten Commandments* to make ten new words.

- Have the children compare their lists.

- Invite the children to figure out how many unique words they have come up with.

Prepare

✓ Provide a CD of upbeat Christian music and a CD player.

Musical Numbers

- Have the children stand in a circle.

- **Say:** When the music begins, start walking in a circle. When the music ends, I will call out a number between one and ten. Form groups with the number of people that corresponds to the number I called out.

- Let the children know which direction to walk.

- Begin playing music.

- Stop the music and call out a number. Encourage the children to form groups as directed.

- Invite any child who is not in a group to share with the class one thing God wants us to do.

- After all children who are not in a group have shared, have the children form a circle again.

- Repeat the process calling out a different number each time.

- **Say:** Our Bible story today is about some rules that help us know how God wants us to live.

Moses: Children's Leader Guide

Large Group

Bring all the children together to experience the Bible story. Use a bell to alert the children to the large-group time.

Ten Things Ten Times

- **Say:** I am going to give you ten commands. Each time I tell you to do something, do that thing ten times.

- Give the following commands and encourage the children to do each action ten times.
    - Clap
    - Stomp
    - Pat your knees
    - Snap with your one hand
    - Snap with your other hand
    - Hop on one foot
    - Hop on the other foot
    - Pat your head
    - Jump
    - March

Moses' Story

- **Say:** We have been hearing stories about Moses' life. Last week we heard about Moses leading the Israelites out of Egypt where they had been slaves for over four hundred years. When the Israelites left Egypt they had to learn to trust God. Today we are going to hear about some rules God gave the Israelites.

- Invite your recruited volunteer to help you tell the story from **Reproducible 4a: The Ten Commandments.**

- **Say:** These are the commandments that God gave to the Israelites to help them live with each other.

- **Ask:** Do you think these commandments apply to us today? Are these commandments for everyone or just for some people?

- **Say:** God's commandments are for everyone to follow. They help us know how to treat God and how to treat each other. Even though it has been thousands of years since God first gave the commandments to the Israelites, they still apply to us today.

Prepare

✓ Provide copies of **Reproducible 4a: The Ten Commandments**.

✓ Recruit a volunteer to come and read the story of Moses each week. *Optional*: If Bible-times costumes are available, have your volunteer dress as a shepherd.

✓ *Note*: This week you will read the parts of the story in bold type.

Prepare

✓ Write this week's Bible verse on a markerboard or a piece of mural paper and place it where it can easily be seen. ("I am the LORD your God." Exodus 20:2a)

Prepare

✓ Display the posters made earlier in the "Rules, Rules, Rules" activity where the children will be able to see them.

✓ Have available a copy of **Reproducible 4a: The Ten Commandments**.

Emphasize the Bible Verse

• Show the Bible verse.

• Encourage the children to read the verse together with you.

• **Ask:** Who said these words? (God)

• **Say:** We are going to say the Bible verse six more times. Each time we say the verse we will stress a different word. The first time we say the verse we will put the emphasis on the first word: *I*. The second time we say the verse we will put the emphasis on the second word: *am*. We will continue until we have stressed each word in the verse.

• Encourage the children to say the Bible verse with you six times, emphasizing a different word each time.

How God Wants Us to Live

• **Say:** Earlier some of you came up with a list of rules.

• Show the children the posters.

• **Say:** You came up with a lot of rules.

• **Ask:** Why do we have rules? Does every family or school have the same rules? Who makes the rules? What do you think life would be like if there were no rules?

• **Say:** Today we heard about God's rules. We call these rules commandments. These rules were first given to Moses and the Israelites thousands of years ago. They still apply to us today. I am going to read the commandments to you one more time. As you listen to each commandment this time, think about whether the commandment tells us how to treat God or if it tells us how to treat other people. If the commandment relates to God, stand up. If the commandment relates to other people, sit down.

• Read each commandment from **Reproducible 4a: The Ten Commandments**. You will only read the numbered sentences. Allow children time to respond by standing or sitting.

• **Say:** The first four commandments address our relationship with God. The last six commandments address our relationship with other people. God gave us these commandments because God loves us and wants us to know how to be in relationship with God and others.

• **Pray:** God, thank you for loving us. Thank you for giving us rules that remind us how you want us to live. Help us to follow your commandments. Amen.

• Dismiss children to their small groups.

Small Groups

Divide the children into small groups. You may organize the groups around age levels or around readers and nonreaders. Keep the groups small, with a maximum of ten children in each group. You may need to have more than one group of each age level.

Young Children

- **Say:** Let's play a game to review the commandments we've heard today. I am going to read a list of rules. If the rule is a commandment, jump up and say, "Ding, ding, ding!" If the rule is not a commandment, stay seated and say, "Buzz!"
- Read the following statements and encourage the children to respond.
  - o   Do not talk with your mouth full. (Buzz)
  - o   There is only one God. (Ding, Ding, Ding)
  - o   Raise your hand before speaking. (Buzz)
  - o   Do not hit your brother. (Buzz)
  - o   Honor your father and your mother. (Ding, Ding, Ding)
  - o   Do not steal. (Ding, Ding, Ding)
  - o   Look both ways before crossing the street. (Buzz)
  - o   Do not want what others have. (Ding, Ding, Ding)
  - o   Do not put chewing gum under your chair. (Buzz)
  - o   Only use God's name when you are talking about God or praying to God. (Ding, Ding, Ding)
  - o   Remember the Sabbath day and keep it holy. (Ding, Ding, Ding)
  - o   Say please and thank you. (Buzz)
  - o   Eat your vegetables. (Buzz)
  - o   Do not murder. (Ding, Ding, Ding)
  - o   Remember to brush your teeth every day. (Buzz)
  - o   Worship only God. (Ding, Ding, Ding)
  - o   Do not commit adultery. (Ding, Ding, Ding)
- **Say:** Just because something isn't a commandment doesn't mean it isn't a good idea. But the commandments God gave us are the most important rules. Let's add a page about the commandments to the book we have been making about Moses.
- Show the children the posterboard you have prepared.
- Encourage the children to work together to plan an illustration to go along with the words. One possibility is to write the numbers one through ten. Have the children draw the picture.
- Tape the new piece of posterboard onto the back of the book.
- **Say:** As you are going through your week, remember to live as God wants you to live by following God's commandments.
- **Pray:** God, help us to follow your commandments so that we are living as you want us to live. Thank you for loving us. Amen.
- Save the big book to be used next week.

Prepare

- ✓ Provide a piece of posterboard, markers, crayons, and masking tape.
- ✓ Supply the big book of *Lessons from the Life of Moses* started three weeks ago.
- ✓ Use a marker to write the following words at the bottom of a piece of posterboard, leaving room above the words for illustrations: "God gives us rules to help us know how to act."

Prepare

✓ Provide paper, pencils, markers, and crayons.

✓ Supply the story cube the children have been working on.

Older Children

- **Say:** Today we are talking about God's Ten Commandments.

- Give each child a piece of paper and a pencil.

- **Say:** Let's play a silly game. Pretend that you are able to make an eleventh commandment. Maybe your commandment would say that you could only eat donuts on Thursdays. Or perhaps it would say you could not wear purple shirts in the winter.

- Encourage children to write an eleventh commandment on their piece of paper without letting anyone else see it.

- Collect all the papers.

- Read each eleventh commandment one at a time. After reading each commandment invite children to guess who wrote the commandment. Affirm each child's work.

- **Say:** Those were some interesting commandments. It is fun to be silly. God gave us the real commandments so we would know how to treat God and how to treat each other. Let's add to the story cube we've been making.

- Have the children turn to a blank side of the cube and write the words, "God gives us rules to help us know how to act." Let the children decorate this side of the box.

- **Say:** As you are going through your week, remember to live as God wants you to live by following God's commandments.

- **Pray:** God, thank you for your love for us. We love you and want to follow your commandments. Help us to live as you want us to as we look for ways to do your work. Amen.

- Save the story cube to be used next week.

The Ten Commandments

Hello! It's me, Moses. Last week I told you about God freeing the Israelites. After we left Egypt, we were living in the wilderness, learning to trust God, and learning how to live with each other now that we were free. God gave me some rules for the people to follow to help them know how to treat God and each other. These are the Ten Commandments God gave us.

1. I am the Lord your God. You must have no other gods before me.
In other words: There is only one God.

2. Do not make an idol for yourself of anything in the sky, on the earth, or in the water.
In other words: Do not make anything more important than God.

3. Do not use the Lord your God's name as if it were of no significance.
In other words: God's name is special; use it only when you are talking about God or praying to God.

4. Remember the Sabbath day and treat it as holy.
In other words: Sunday is a special day set aside to rest and worship God.

5. Honor your father and your mother.
In other words: Treat your parents with love and respect.

6. Do not kill.
In other words: God gives life; it is wrong to take that away from anyone.

7. Do not commit adultery.
In other words: Marriage is a special commitment between two people.

8. Do not steal.
In other words: Do not take things that don't belong to you.

9. Do not testify falsely against your neighbor.
In other words: Do not tell lies about other people.

10. Do not wish you had the things someone else has.
In other words: Be grateful for what you have instead of wanting what others have.

Based on Exodus 19:1–20:21

5. In the Wilderness

Objectives

The children will:

- hear the story of Moses and the Israelites wandering in the wilderness
- discover that God was with the Israelites in the wilderness.
- explore God's presence in their own lives.

Bible Story

The Israelites in the Wilderness
Exodus 15:22–17:7

Bible Verse

"God said, 'I'll be with you.'"

Exodus 3:12

Focus for the Teacher

The Israelites had been freed from the slavery they experienced for over four hundred years. One might reasonably expect that once they were free they would have been happy. But as today's story illustrates, change is difficult. Even change for the better is stressful. The Israelites were not used to living in freedom and trusting God to provide for their needs.

God had led Moses and the rest of the Israelites out of Egypt and across the Reed Sea. They were not yet to the Promised Land of milk and honey. Instead they found themselves in the wilderness. The wilderness was a precarious place. The people's need for food and water were real and neither was abundant in this desert landscape. The people became anxious. In their anxiety, they began to complain and wish they had never left Egypt. How quickly they had forgotten their oppression under Pharaoh's hand. At least in Egypt there was food to eat and water to drink. Their fear and anxiety distorted their memory of what life had been like in Egypt.

Just as God had heard their cries and rescued them from slavery in Egypt, God again

> God provides for our needs in good times and bad times.

responded to their complaints. God provided for their needs, sending quail in the evening and manna in the morning. It is important to note that God provided just what they needed and no more. Each person, regardless of how much manna he or she collected, ended up with the same amount. Some Israelites did not trust God to continue to provide manna every day so they tried to take matters into their own hands and save some. The excess manna stank and became infested with worms. But fresh manna appeared every day to meet their needs.

Except on the Sabbath. Even when traveling through the wilderness, the importance of resting on the Sabbath was to be observed. No manna appeared on that day, but the day before the Sabbath was the one time extra manna could be stored without it rotting.

God provided the Israelites with what they needed. When the manna was distributed equally, everyone had enough. There was no need to hoard or be greedy. There is much for us to learn from this story if we are willing to pay attention.

Explore Interest Groups

Be sure that adult leaders are waiting when the first child arrives. Greet and welcome each child. Get the children involved in an activity that interests them and introduces the theme for the day's activities.

Sand Picture

- Show the children the colored sand.

- **Ask:** Where might you find a lot of sand—in a jungle or a desert? (a desert)

- **Say:** Today we are going to hear a story about Moses and the Israelites spending time in the desert. They probably saw a lot of sand though it wasn't colored like this sand. You are going to use this sand to make a picture.

- Give each child a copy of **Reproducible 5a: Sand Picture**.

- Have each child place their picture in a shallow tray or box.

- Encourage each child to use glue to outline a few of the letters on the page.

- Let each child use a spoon to sprinkle sand on top of the glue.

- Have each child pick up the picture and gently shake off the excess sand into the tray or box.

- Invite each child to continue tracing letters, sprinkling sand, and shaking off excess sand until the picture is complete. Children may add extra designs to their pictures also.

- Let the pictures dry.

Prepare

✓ Provide copies of **Reproducible 5a: Sand Picture** on cardstock for each child.

✓ Supply glue, colored sand, plastic containers, spoons, and shallow trays or boxes.

✓ Pour each color of sand into a separate container.

Silly Complaint Game

- Have the children sit in a circle.

- **Ask**: What is a complaint? (finding fault and saying something negative)

- **Say:** It seems like some people like to complain about everything. We don't usually encourage complaining, but today we are going to play a game to see how many silly complaints we can come up with about the weather today. I will start by saying, "It's not cold enough!" We'll go around the circle. The next person will say, "It's not cold enough and . . ." and add another silly complaint. Each person will repeat all the previous complaints and add another one. The sillier the better! Let's see how long and silly we can make our list of complaints.

- Play the game with the children.

- **Say:** In the Bible story for today we will hear some complaining.

Prepare

✓ *Note*: Remind the children to complain about the weather and avoid making complaints about people.

Prepare

✓ Find a large clear wall space in your classroom or elsewhere in the church for the children to use for this project.

✓ Use a marker to write "Give Thanks" on a piece of paper.

✓ Supply yarn, tape, and scissors.

✓ *Tip*: If there is no wall space available, the children can spell out the words on the floor. Make sure to pick up the yarn at the end of the activity to prevent anyone from tripping.

Spell It Out

• **Say:** In today's Bible story, we will hear about the Israelites complaining to Moses.

• **Ask:** Have you ever complained about something?

• **Say:** Like the Israelites, we sometimes complain. When we complain we are focusing on the negative. When we do that we forget all the reasons we have to be positive. Today you are going to make a big reminder to focus on the positive and give thanks for what we have.

• Show the children the clear wall space.

• Give the children the yarn and have them work together to spell out the words, "Give Thanks" on the wall, using tape to secure the yarn as needed. Let the children use the words you have written as a spelling guide.

• Encourage the children to make the letters as large as possible and still have the words fit in the space available.

Prepare

✓ Write the words, "Thank you, God," vertically down the left side of a piece of paper. Make copies of the page for each child.

✓ Supply pencils.

Thankful Acrostic

• Give each child a copy of the acrostic form you have made.

• **Say:** An acrostic is a type of poem made up of words or phrases that begin with the letters in a particular word or phrase.

• Encourage children to think of things they are thankful for.

• Invite each child to write a thankful acrostic by writing a word or phrase about something they are thankful for that begins with each letter on the paper.

• Let the children share their acrostics with each other.

Large Group

Bring all the children together to experience the Bible story. Use a bell to alert the children to the large-group time.

Thankful Rhythm

- Have the children sit in a circle.
- **Say:** It is always good to give thanks to God. Right now I want you to think of three things you are thankful for.
- Give the children a few moments to think of three things.
- **Say:** We are going to thank God while we play a rhythm game. The rhythm we will do is tapping our knees with our hands two times, clapping two times and then snapping two times, once with each hand. Let's try it.
- Lead the children in doing the rhythm a couple of times.
- **Say:** Now we will add words. As we pat we will say, "Thank you". As we clap we will say, "God, for". And as we snap one person will say one of the things he or she is thankful for. The next time we do the rhythm, the person to the left of that person will share, and we will continue around the circle. Let's see if we can make it all the way around the circle while keeping our rhythm going.
- Choose a person to start and play the game.
- **Say:** Giving thanks is a good way to focus on the positive things in our lives.

Prepare

✓ Cut a large sheet of mural paper and tape it to the wall where the children can easily see it.

✓ Draw a vertical line down the middle of the paper. At the top of the left-hand column write the word *Reassurance*. At the top of the right-hand column write the word *Responsibility*.

Personalize the Bible Verse

- Show the children the Bible verse
- Encourage the children to say the Bible verse with you.
- **Say:** God said these words to Moses when he spoke to him from the burning bush. Moses had to remind the Israelites many times that God had promised to be with them.
- **Ask:** Is God with us?
- **Say:** Of course! Just as God was with Moses and the Israelites, God is also with us. We are going to say the verse one more time. This time when we say the verse, add your name on the end. For example, I will say, "God said, 'I'll be with you, (your name).'"
- Encourage the children to say the verse with you, with everyone saying their own name.

Prepare

✓ Write this week's Bible verse on a markerboard or a piece of mural paper and place it where it can easily be seen. ("God said, 'I'll be with you.'" Exodus 3:12)

Prepare

✓ Provide copies of **Reproducible 5b: The Israelites in the Wilderness**.

✓ Recruit a volunteer to come and read the story of Moses each week. *Optional*: If Bible times costumes are available, have your volunteer dress as a shepherd.

✓ Invite several confident readers to help tell the Bible story. Give each reader a copy of the story. Encourage the readers to follow along as Moses tells the story. Have the readers read the words in bold type in unison.

Moses' Story

- **Say:** We are continuing to hear Moses' story. We have heard how God called Moses to lead the Israelites out of slavery in Egypt. Last week we heard about the commandments God gave the Israelites to help them learn to live as free people. Today we will hear about something else that happened after the Israelites left Egypt.

- Invite your recruited volunteers to tell the story from **Reproducible 5b: The Israelites in the Wilderness.**

- Thank your volunteers for telling the story.

- **Ask:** What were the Israelites complaining about? (not having food and water) How did they get water and food? (God provided it.)

- **Say:** The Israelites had been slaves for a long time. They weren't used to trusting God to provide the things they needed. God took care of the Israelites in the wilderness. While the Israelites were busy complaining, they weren't noticing the ways God was providing for them.

God Cares for All People

- **Say:** When we get in the mood to complain like the Israelites did, we can stop and remember to be thankful instead. We have many things to be thankful for and we've mentioned some of them already. We can always give thanks that God is with us and God cares for us. We are going to say a litany together. I will read a statement. Your response is, "God cares for all people."

- Have the children practice their response.

- Lead the children in the following litany.
  - o **Leader**: When the Israelites were thirsty, God provided water. God took care of the Israelites.
  - o **All**: God cares for all people.
  - o **Leader**: When the Israelites were hungry, God provided manna and quail for them to eat. God took care of the Israelites.
  - o **All**: God cares for all people.
  - o **Leader**: God provided for the Israelites. God provides for us.
  - o **All**: God cares for all people.
  - o **Leader**: Instead of complaining, we choose to give thanks that God is with us.
  - o **All**: God cares for all people.

- **Pray:** Thank you, God, for loving us and caring for us. Help us to share your love as we care for each other. Amen.

- Dismiss children to their small groups.

Small Groups

Divide the children into small groups. You may organize the groups around age levels or around readers and nonreaders. Keep the groups small, with a maximum of ten children in each group. You may need to have more than one group of each age level.

Young Children

- Show the children the book *Lessons from the Life of Moses*.
- Read the book, encouraging the children to review the stories and share what they remember.
- Show the children the posterboard you have prepared.
- Encourage the children to work together to plan an illustration to go along with the words. One possibility is the Israelites collecting manna in baskets. Have the children draw the picture.
- Tape the new piece of posterboard onto the back of the book.
- **Say:** Sometimes it is easy to focus on complaining like the Israelites did instead of remembering the good things in our lives. We may not have everything we want, but we have many things.
- Give each child a piece of paper.
- **Say:** Let's spend some time focusing on the things we do have.
- Have the children fold their papers in half bringing the short sides together. Then have them fold their papers in half again in the same direction.
- Encourage each child to unfold the paper, now divided into four sections.
- Give the children the following instructions, allowing time for them to draw:
  - o In one of the sections of your paper, draw a picture of someone who loves you.
  - o In another section, draw a picture of your favorite food.
  - o In another section, draw a picture of your favorite piece of clothing.
  - o In the last section, draw a picture of where you live.
- **Say:** You have just shown some of the ways God provides and cares for you. These are things you can be thankful for.
- **Pray:** God, thank you for the many ways you care for us. Amen.
- Save the big book to be used next week.

Prepare

✓ Provide a piece of posterboard, markers, crayons, masking tape, and paper.

✓ Supply the big book of *Lessons from the Life of Moses*.

✓ Use a marker to write the following words at the bottom of a piece of posterboard, leaving room above the words for illustrations: "God is with us!"

Prepare

✓ Provide markers, crayons, and mural paper.

✓ Supply the story cube the children have been working on.

✓ Cut a large piece of mural paper.

Older Children

- **Say:** We have been making a story cube to help us remember the lessons from Moses' life. Let's review what we've learned so far.

- Encourage the children look at the story cube and work together to review the previous lessons.

- Have the children turn to the last blank side of the cube and write the words, "God is with us! God cares for us!" Let the children decorate this side of the box.

- Have the children sit in a circle. Place the mural paper in the center of the circle.

- **Say:** God performed many powerful acts to free the Israelites from slavery in Egypt. At first the people praised God for the things God had done. It didn't take long for the people to start complaining again. It was as though they'd already forgotten the many things God had done for them.

- **Ask:** Why do you think people find it easy to complain about things?

- Allow children an opportunity to share their ideas.

- **Say:** The thing about complaining is that it is easy to get caught up in the process of whining and forget about the good things that are happening. That's what happened to the Israelites. It can happen to us too. One way to minimize complaining is to focus on the good things. Sometimes we call that counting our blessings. Let's do some brainstorming.

- **Ask:** What are your blessings?

- As the children name blessings, jot a word or two down on the mural paper as a reminder of each thing named.

- Encourage the children to count the blessings that have been named.

- **Say:** That's a lot of blessings! Focusing on the good things in our lives reminds us how God cares for us.

- **Pray:** God, thank you for the many ways you care for us. Help us to focus on our blessings rather than on complaining. Amen.

- Save the story cube to be used next week.

Sand Picture

GOD IS WITH ME.

The Israelites in the Wilderness

Hello! Moses here. Today I'm going to tell you about the time after God freed the Israelites from slavery in Egypt.

After God parted the Reed Sea so we could escape from Pharaoh's army, God led us into the desert. We traveled for three days in the desert and found no water. When we finally came to a place with water, we couldn't drink it because it was too bitter. The people came to me and complained.

"We're thirsty! What will we drink?"

I told God the Israelites' complaint, and God showed me a tree. When I threw a branch from the tree into the water, the water became sweet and the people were able to drink it.

As we continued to travel in the wilderness, the people became hungry but there was no food. Once again, the people came to me and complained.

"We're hungry! We wish we were back in Egypt. At least there was food to eat there!"

God told me, "I'm going to make bread come down from the sky for you. And I will provide meat for you in the evenings."

God provided for the Israelites as promised. Each evening quail flew in and covered the camp so there was meat for the people to eat. And in the mornings, manna—bread from heaven—covered the ground.

God instructed us to collect one omer of manna each morning, and that would provide the food needed for the day. When the people went out to collect manna, some collected more and some collected less. But when they measured it out, every person had one omer—just what they needed.

Some people tried to collect extra manna and store it, but the extra manna spoiled and became infested with worms.

On the sixth day, the people each collected two omers of manna because this is what God instructed. This was so they didn't have to collect manna on the Sabbath. No manna appeared on the Sabbath because God wanted us to rest.

The Israelites were in the wilderness for forty years before we came to the land God promised us. God provided for us the entire time, making sure we had what we needed. Even when the people forgot to trust God and complained, God was with us.

Based on Exodus 15:22–17:7

6. Remember and Pass It On

Objectives

The children will:

- hear the Shema.
- discover that Moses encouraged people to remember and tell stories about God.
- explore the importance of telling stories of their faith.

Bible Story

The Shema
Deuteronomy 6:4-9

Bible Verse

These words that I am commanding you today must always be on your minds.

Deuteronomy 6:6

Focus for the Teacher

During this study we have been hearing the stories of Moses. We have seen that Moses was not perfect. Moses was human; he made mistakes. Sometimes Moses was reluctant to do what God asked. God called Moses, imperfect as he was, to do God's work. Moses was an important prophet and an influential leader. As we remember the stories we've heard and the lessons we've learned, it is appropriate that the final lesson to learn from Moses' life is to remember.

The Israelites were in the wilderness for forty years before entering Canaan, the land God had promised to bring them to. The Israelites preparing to enter Canaan were not the same Israelites that had been slaves in Egypt. This was a new generation of Israelites. They had not witnessed firsthand God's powerful acts to free them from slavery and bring them safely out of Egypt. As Moses addressed this new generation of Israelites poised to enter the Promised Land, he once again recited the story. He reminded them again of how God had brought them this far. He reminded them of the commandments God gave them. Then Moses

> We should remember these stories and pass them on.

told them to remember these stories and pass them on.

Today's Bible story is a teaching known as the Shema. *Shema* is the Hebrew word for hear or listen, which is the first word of this Scripture passage. In Matthew's Gospel when Jesus was asked which commandment is the greatest, he replied with the words of the Shema. When Moses spoke the words of the Shema to the Israelites, he went on to stress the importance of these words by instructing the Israelites to recite these words to their children, to talk about them at home and away, in the morning and at night.

Additionally, the words are to be put in a place where they will frequently be seen, on their hands and foreheads and on their doorframes. Observant Jews follow these instructions by including the Shema in their morning and evening prayers. Whether we recite these words twice a day, or post them on our doorframe, the underlying message is that we are to constantly think about and act upon the commandment that we are to love God. And as we remember these words and stories, we are also to pass them on.

Moses: Children's Leader Guide

Explore Interest Groups

Be sure that adult leaders are waiting when the first child arrives. Greet and welcome each child. Get the children involved in an activity that interests them and introduces the theme for the day's activities.

Make Banners

- Give each child a piece of paper.
- Let each child choose one of the index cards you have prepared.
- **Say:** We are going to work together to make a banner. Each of you will write the word you've been given on your piece of paper. You may use bubble letters or fancy writing, but make the letters big so people will be able to read the word.
- Encourage each child to write and decorate their assigned word.
- Help the children lay the pages in the correct order to form a long banner reading, "Love the LORD your God with all your heart, all your being, and all your strength."
- Tape the pages together.
- Find a place to display the banner and let the children help you hang it up.
- **Say:** We will hear these words when we hear our Bible story from Moses today.

Prepare

- ✓ Write each word of the following verse on a separate index card: "Love the LORD your God with all your heart, all your being, and all your strength."
- ✓ Provide paper, markers, and tape.
- ✓ *Tip*: If you have fewer than sixteen children, invite some children to make more than one poster. If you have more than sixteen children, have children work together or make multiple sets of index cards and make more than one banner.

People Who Love God

- **Say:** We are going to play a game about people who love God.
- Choose one child to stand in the center of the circle of chairs, and have the rest of the children sit in the chairs.
- Explain the following rules to the children:
  - o The person in the center will describe people who love God using a characteristic that describes himself or herself. For example, if I have short hair I might say, "People who have short hair love God." If I am wearing blue I might say, "People who are wearing blue love God."
  - o Every person in the circle for whom that statement is true must get up and find a new seat that is not right next to where he or she has been sitting while the person in the middle tries to get a seat also.
  - o The person left standing becomes the next person to describe people who love God.
  - o If the person in the center says, "Everybody loves God," then everyone must get up and find a new seat.
- Encourage the children to play the game.

Prepare

- ✓ Form a circle of chairs facing inward, using one less chair than the number of children in your class.

Prepare

✓ Place a variety of small items on a tray. Some suggestions: crayon, penny, bandage, cotton ball, paper clip, piece of string, marker, eraser, rubber band, scissors.

✓ Cover the tray of items with a towel.

✓ Provide paper and pencils.

Test Your Memory

- Uncover the items on the tray and show them to the children.

- **Say:** Take a good look at the things I've collected.

- Place the towel back over the items.

- Give each child a piece of paper and a pencil.

- **Say:** Try to remember everything that was on the tray and write them on your paper.

- Give children a few moments to write.

- Have the children put their pencils down.

- Remove the towel and let the children look at the items again.

- Replace the towel and let the children continue making their lists of the objects on the tray.

- Let the children look at the objects several more times until it appears most children have remembered most of the objects. The number of times will depend on the number of items on the tray and the age of the children.

- Take the towel off of the objects and let the children compare their lists to the items on the tray.

- **Ask:** How did you do at remembering what was on the tray? What made it challenging to remember? Did it get easier to remember the more times you were able to look at the objects?

- **Say:** When we see something multiple times we are more likely to remember it. The same is true of stories that we hear. The more times we hear a story, the more we remember it.

Moses: Children's Leader Guide

Large Group

Bring all the children together to experience the Bible story. Use a bell to alert the children to the large-group time.

Love God Cheer

- Lead the children in the following cheer:
  - o **Leader**: Give me an L!
  - o **All**: L!
  - o **Leader**: Give me an O!
  - o **All**: O!
  - o **Leader**: Give me a V!
  - o **All**: V!
  - o **Leader**: Give me an E!
  - o **All**: E!
  - o **Leader**: What's that spell?
  - o **All**: Love!
  - o **Leader**: Give me a G!
  - o **All**: G!
  - o **Leader**: Give me an O!
  - o **All**: O!
  - o **Leader**: Give me a D!
  - o **All**: D!
  - o **Leader**: What's that spell?
  - o **All**: God!
  - o **Leader**: Put the two words together!
  - o **All**: Love God!

Moses' Story

- **Say:** We have been hearing stories from Moses. He has one more story to tell us.
- Invite your recruited volunteer to tell the story from **Reproducible 6a: The Shema.**
- Thank your volunteer for telling the story.
- **Say:** Part of the story we just heard is known as the Shema. Listen again to these words.
- Read the quotation from The Shema that begins, "Israel, listen!"
- **Ask:** What does it mean to love God with all your heart? (to be faithful) What does it mean to love God with all your being? (to love God more than anything) What does it mean to love God with all your strength? (to serve God as much as you can)
- **Say:** These words were written thousands of years ago but are still important. These words continue to be taught. That's why we are learning them today.

Prepare

- ✓ Provide copies of **Reproducible 6a: The Shema.**

- ✓ Recruit a volunteer to come and read the story of Moses each week. *Optional*: If Bible times costumes are available, have your volunteer dress as a shepherd.

Remember and Pass It On

Prepare

✓ Write this week's Bible verse on a markerboard or a piece of mural paper and place it where it can easily be seen. ("These words that I am commanding you today must always be on your minds." Deuteronomy 6:6)

Control the Volume of the Bible Verse

• Show the Bible verse.

• Encourage the children to read the verse together with you.

• **Say:** Now let's pretend I am a volume control slider. We will read the verse together three more times. When I am standing over here (move all the way to your right side) the volume needs to be very soft. As I walk across the room, the volume increases and when I am standing over here (move all the way to your left side) the volume is very loud.

• Encourage the children to read the verse with you three more times as you control the volume with your position.

Tell the Stories

• **Say:** Moses reminded the Israelites to love God with all their heart, being, and strength. A long time after Moses lived, a man named Jesus was teaching.

• **Ask:** Who was Jesus? (God's Son)

• **Say:** That's right. Jesus was God's Son and he taught people about God and about how God wants us to live. One day when Jesus was teaching, someone asked him what the greatest commandment was. Jesus replied, "You must love the Lord your God with all your heart, with all your being, and with all your mind." (Matthew 22:37)

• **Ask:** Do those words sound familiar?

• **Say:** Jesus answered the question with the words of the Shema. Now Jesus lived hundreds of years after Moses. But Moses had told the Israelites to pass these words to their children. For many generations, parents taught these words to their children and then those children became parents and taught the words to their children. Eventually, Jesus' parents taught them to him.

• **Ask:** Who has taught you about your faith? Who tells you stories about God? Who do you tell about God? Why do you think it's important to remember and share the stories of our faith?

• Allow an opportunity for children to share their thoughts and ideas.

• **Say:** Moses knew that retelling stories helps people remember. Let's keep telling people about God.

• **Pray:** God, thank you for stories that remind us about your love and care for us. Help us to keep telling the stories as we love you with all our heart, being, and strength. Amen.

• Dismiss children to their small groups.

Small Groups

Divide the children into small groups. You may organize the groups around age levels or around readers and nonreaders. Keep the groups small, with a maximum of ten children in each group. You may need to have more than one group of each age level.

Young Children

- **Say:** As we have heard the stories of Moses' life, we have been making a big book.

- Read the book. After you read each page, challenge the children to work together to remember as much as they can about the story that inspired that page.

- **Say:** You did a good job of remembering the stories. That's what we've been talking about today, the importance of telling the stories and remembering them. One of the things Moses told people to do to remember to love God was to write the words of the Shema on their doorframes.

- **Ask:** Why do you think this would help people remember? (because they would see the words often)

- **Say:** You are going to make a poster that you can take home and hang in your room to remind you to love God.

- Give each child a piece of paper.

- Encourage each child to create a poster reminder with the words, "Love God."

- **Say:** When you take your poster home, hang it where you will see it often. It will help you remember to love God.

- **Pray:** God, we love you with all our hearts, all our being, and all our strength. Thank you for stories that teach us about you and help us know how you want us to live. Amen.

Prepare

✓ Supply the big book of *Lessons from the Life of Moses*.

✓ Provide paper, crayons, and markers.

Prepare

✓ Provide the story cube the children have made.

Older Children

- Have the children sit in a circle.

- **Say:** As we have heard the stories of Moses' life, we have made a story cube. Today we've going to use our story cube to review what we've learned.

- Explain the rules of the review game to the children:
  - o One person will turn the story cube around and put it in the center of the circle, choosing which side of the cube to face up.
  - o As the person places the cube in the center of the circle he or she will call out someone's name.
  - o The person whose name was called will read the words on the side of the cube that is facing up and then call out someone else's name.
  - o The person who was called by name will tell us something he or she remembers about the story referred to by the lesson just read. That person will then turn the cube and begin the process again.
  - o If the side of the cube facing up says, *Lessons from the Life of Moses*, then you may choose from any of the stories we've heard to share your remembrance.

- Encourage the children to play the game.

- **Say:** You have done a good job of remembering.

- **Pray:** God, thank you for the stories we have heard about Moses and the lessons they have taught us about you. We love you with all our hearts, all our being, and all our strength. Amen.

The Shema

Hello! Moses here to tell you one more story. I've told you many stories about my life. You've heard about the women that protected my life when I was a baby. I told you about God calling to me from the burning bush. I've shared about going to Egypt and telling Pharaoh to free the Israelites from slavery. What a time that was! Remember how Pharaoh kept changing his mind?

Even after the we left Egypt, Pharaoh chased us. God parted the Reed Sea so we could cross it and escape from Pharaoh's army. Our time in the wilderness was not always easy. I spent a lot of time reminding the Israelites to trust God. Through it all, God was with us. God gave us the Ten Commandments to help us learn to live together. God provided us with food and water while we were living in the wilderness.

So many stories! We lived in the wilderness for forty years before God led us to the land God had promised us. Before the Israelites crossed into the Promised Land, I reminded them of everything we had been through. I spoke about God's faithfulness through everything.

I said, "Israel, listen! Our God is the LORD! Only the LORD! Love the LORD your God with all your heart, all your being, and all your strength. These words I am commanding you today must always be on your minds. Recite them to your children. Talk about them when you are sitting around your house and when you are out and about, when you are lying down and when you are getting up. Tie them on your hand as a sign. They should be on your forehead as a symbol. Write them on your house's doorframes and on your city's gates."

I really wanted the Israelites to remember to love and trust God. Thank you for letting me tell my story to you for the last several weeks. I hope you remember these stories and pass them on.

Based on Deuteronomy 6:4-9